BEYC
Conserving the Land

Series Editor: MEIC STEPHENS

Beyond National Parks

Conserving the Landscape of a Democratic Wales

Ioan Bowen Rees

First Impression—1995

ISBN 1 85902 286 3

Printed in Wales by
J. D. Lewis, and Sons Ltd., Gomer Press, Llandysul, Dyfed

PROLOGUE

Some years ago, in the first week of May, I made three different excursions into the mountains of Gwynedd. Monday took me up the north ridge of Tryfan: the rock was adhesive, the breeze gentle, my own rhythm poised enough to call for little effort on the solid ribs which surmount the crumbling base of the mountain. Whenever a fin of ridge appeared ahead, it was a clean outline against cobalt sky. Content with upward movement and immediate sensation, I could have been on good rock almost anywhere in the world.

On Wednesday, it was Elidir Fawr on a grey day of drifting and lifting cloud. As I descended slippery ledges above Bwlch Marchlyn with visibility down to twenty yards, a window opened in the cloud and there was Bwlch y Brecan opening a further window upon the rosy precipices of Pen yr Ole Wen, with Carnedd Ddafydd beyond. Sometimes I think of Arthur above Marchlyn Mawr, harnessed though it is, and of the folk-lore recounted to John Rhys. This time the cloud effects made me a Caspar David Friedrich foreground figure with symphonic music rolling through his mind: themes rather later, as it happens, than those of Friedrich's time, the winding down of Mahler's Ninth and phrases from the Abschied of the *Lied von der Erde*:

> 'Ich geh, ich wandre in die Berge
> Ich suche Ruhe... Ruhe für mein einsam Herz.'

With so much hidden from view, I could have been anywhere in Europe, or rather any European on almost any mountain below the snowline.

It was after a dip at Dinas Dinlle, in sight of the Eifl, that we decided to take the car as high as possible and walk up Craig

Cwm Silyn. This is familiar ground to me but, from the summit ridge, I hardly recognized Moelwyn Mawr, its peak was so much bolder and closer in the clarity of that sunset, as if Piz Linard had strayed a thousand kilometres from the Engiadina Bassa: in Wales the very weather, the constant variation of scent and tint and light, usually spices the expected. Another reason why the grassy ascent to the Cwm Silyn ridge is less tedious than it looks is that the approach is so evocative: not only was Williams Parry brought up down there in Tal-y-sarn but the farms and ruined cottages scattered around the end of the metalled road include the homes of Silyn, Alun Roberts and Mathonwy. Silyn was a quarryman before going to college in his late twenties: 'a walking flame', he became a pioneer, both of the ILP and of a new wave of Welsh verse: it was at his funeral that Williams Parry visualised death starting with a walk up to the horizon before the 'slow pilgrim' turns to wave a last farewell. (Is there a conscious echo here of the Eighth Duino Elegy, which preceded it by some seven years?) The Professor of Agriculture Alun Roberts's essays on rural life, *Hafodydd Brithion* (also the name of a farm above Nant Gwynant) became a prose classic: it was Williams Parry again who lamented his friend's move from the mountain—and its 'greatness without season'—down to the village of Llanllyfni:

> 'O fynwes hedd i fân sôn
> Pentrefwyr pant yr afon.'

The poet Mathonwy was for years deputy editor of *Y Faner,* whose editor, Gwilym R. Jones (a rather more distinguished poet), was also a product of the quarrying community of Dyffryn Nantlle. Once, when I was in digs in Denbigh, where *Y Faner* was published, the two gave me a lift in an old Morris 8 to Conwy, where we were taking part in a Brains Trust: they conversed with one another in perfect *cynghanedd* the whole way, probably to impress me that there was more to education than an Oxford degree. Gwilym R.'s best-known poem is 'Cwm Tawelwch'— 'the valley of stillness' or, literally, 'silence'. It is, however, Williams Parry's 'Dyffryn Nantlle Ddoe a Heddiw' which possesses me whenever I look down northwards from the Nantlle ridge: the poem contrasts the vanished Wales of the Mabinogion with the Wales of the Dorothea Quarry and of 'Salem, Nasareth and Cesarea'—it is from Lleu that Dyffryn Nant*lleu* takes its name, it was for Lleu that the magician Gwydion made a wife, Blodeuwedd, out of flowers, and it was under an oak-tree at this end of Llyn Nantlle that Gwydion turned Lleu back into a man instead of the decrepit eagle he had become after a magical blow from Blodeuwedd's lover—this must be the oak which appears in the foreground of Richard Wilson's Snowdon, a conical view almost formal enough, as a print, to anticipate Hokusai a little, and yet become a Welsh ikon.

The first version of Wilson's painting was exhibited at the Royal Academy in 1766 and almost certainly acquired by William Vaughan of Corsygedol, then President of the Honourable Society of Cymmrodorion. That evening on the summit of Craig Cwm Silyn, contemplating the mountains of Ardudwy above Corsygedol across the bay, it struck me that, environmentally at least, William Vaughan's Wales had more in common with the Wales of the Mabinogion than with Williams Parry's. And yet... down at my feet Cwm Pennant had recently sheltered not only the shepherd of Eifion Wyn's all too familiar poem but also, for four years, Jim Perrin, the kind of Manchester rock-climber who commands almost as much magic as Gwydion and who can—in Jim's case—quote Parry-Williams as he describes 'a landscape where every field-corner was thick with ghosts:'

> '*Mae lleisiau a drychiolaethau ar hyd y lle.*'

Those 'voices and phantoms' now include the ghosts of old mountaineers. At the turn of the century, Archer Thomson, head of a Caernarfonshire county secondary school and one of the pioneer climbers, was always conscious, on the rocks, of the old Arthurian lore. His friend Humphrey Owen Jones's library included O.M. Edwards's editions of the Welsh classics: H.O. Jones was the youngest Fellow of the Royal Society of his day as well as a brilliant Alpinist but neither science nor magic could restore him and his wife Muriel Gwendolen—climber, scientist and folk-singer—after their fall on Mont Rouge de Peuterey, fourteen days after their wedding at Bangor: they were buried at Courmayeur. I should like to have met Humphrey's little sister, Bronwen Ceridwen, another of the first women rock-climbers, perhaps a Blodeuwedd of crystal, moss campion and *Lloydia serotina*. What would she have made of Eric Jones lecturing at Rhyd-ddu to Clwb Mynydda Cymru, in the naturally eloquent Welsh of a Derwen farmer's son, about his renowned solo winter ascent of the Eiger North Wall? Or his early para-glide from the summit of Yr Wyddfa to Dinas Dinlle? The mountaineer's Wales, at least, has a toe-hold in the Mabinogion.

Rhyd-ddu, under the eastern prow of the Nantlle ridge, is even more Parry-Williams than Grasmere is Wordsworth: in his youth, it was only to the mountains that he wished to 'sing his discontent.' Looking southwards to the wealth of association around Llanfrothen, or westwards to the saints' ways over the seas, I could only have been in Wales. It would have been the same above Pwllderi or on Mynydd Preseli, on the Black Mountain and in the Black Mountains, in dozens of places in a Wales in which, even to an essentially Valleys historian like Dai Smith, 'any definition of... experience, native or otherwise, is inseparable from a sense of place.' Ridiculous as it may seem to turn from sublime landscape to legislation, that—as well as her unique natural environment—is why Wales needed a Countryside Council of her own. But is the system of landscape conservation which a Welsh Countryside Council has now taken over from the Countryside Commission based at Cheltenham itself compatible with the identity of Wales, with the needs and rights of the Welsh people and with their common human duty to posterity? For many years, the term Snowdonia has been used to translate the original name of the high mountain core of northern Gwynedd, Eryri. Words can rarely be divorced from their own languages and associations, however, even—on the authority of Walter Benjamin—words as simple as *pain* and *brot*. Neither Eryri nor Snowdonia is a full translation of the other. *Parc Cenedlaethol*, now shown, after protests, on the Ordnance Maps, below the English, in brackets and in smaller print, fails to convey the full meaning of National Park, a term coined, not only in a different language but in a different period and in a different milieu. If it did convey to them the original English associations, let alone those of the American original, how acceptable would it be to the people of Gwynedd?

NATIONAL PARKS

The Welsh landscape is unique, its conservation essential to the economy of Wales and to her very identity: not so much because of the importance of tourism, or the way in which the economic development officers of Dyfed and Gwynedd have to offer quality of life in mitigation of poor communications with the mass-market; but because quality of life, infused with self-respect and sense of identity, retains and stimulates native talent. If the history of the *organized* movement for conserving the Welsh landscape goes back to the thirties at least, it has been dominated by people who view Wales as an escape from the reality of the English conurbations rather than something real in itself. The movement tends to be nostalgic, not only in aims but also in means. Its flagship is still the National Park, its main concern the extent to which the legislation of 1949, 1963 and 1972 failed to fulfil the objectives of the pre-war Standing Committee on National Parks, its ethos centralist Fabian merging into patrician Tory, with a less Olympian wing still fighting (against harassed small farmers) battles won long ago against great English landlords for the right to roam the Pennine grouse-moors. It was fitting indeed that Lord Norrie's recent abortive Bill to create National Park Boards commenced in the House of Lords and that so many distinguished old warriors—several of whom I know and admire—rode their hobby-horses again in a Second Reading session of shameless mutual admiration which was—in the absence of knowledgeable sceptics—anything but a debate.

Not that the underlying aims and enthusiasms of their speeches were anything but admirable: the point is that National Park

Boards will make virtually no difference to their fulfilment, that National Parks as such, any conceivable National Parks on the present lines, are only minor administrative variations on a defective system. To realize that, it matters not whether you have walked every inch of the Pembrokeshire Coastal Path (opened when the same officers served the county council and the National Park). What you need to have done, year after year, is to attend National Park committees, sub-committees, negotiations, conferences, together with the non-National Park equivalents, and, year after year, compare the results on the ground, preferably around your own home. Having been proud to be associated, in a small way, with the excellent work (on the whole) of two National Park Committees, it seemed to me that—given the same resources—they would have done just as well within regular local government. In and around the English Establishment, however, irrespective of party, it is not done to question the sanctity of National Parks. The same could be said about the more egalitarian recreational Establishment. (The former add titles to their names, the latter dispense with surnames.) In Wales too, we tend to be for National Parks, or at least to hold our tongues and make the best of them. This is all very well when one is thinking of the actual mountains of Eryri, or of the Brecon Beacons themselves or of the Pembrokeshire coast. It is a different matter when, by an insidious slip of the mind, one pays to a mere administrative or publicity device—a Board, a committee, a line on the map, an estate agent's plug, a claim on the label of a bottle of spring water—the respect due to the magnificence after which these devices were named. Sometimes, one begins to feel that Snowdon's main claim to fame is to be 'in the Snowdonia National Park.' 'Not this,' cried R.S. Thomas in his search for Abercuawg, 'This is the name, not the thing that the name stands for.'

At an impressionable age, I too came under the spell of the name, 'National Park.' Quite apart from the awe evoked by accounts of real National Parks in virgin territory like Yellowstone in Wyoming, the first National Park of all, the dream of an expatriate Scot, the saints of the English and Welsh

Standing Committee were revered in my own home. I still have my parents' copy of the Committee's *Case for National Parks in Great Britain,* published in July, 1938, price 2d. G.M. Trevelyan, the liberal historian who wrote the foreword, was one of my father's heroes. So was Julian Huxley, who represented on the committee the 'Zoological Society and Society for Protection of the Fauna of the Empire.' After the War, it was my mother who founded—or at least revived—our county branch of CPRW (Council for the Preservation of Rural Wales, as it then was) and who led a successful campaign to keep Cwm Cau on Cadair Idris, the most perfect cwm in Wales, out of the clutches of the electricity generators: in the early 'fifties, it was the mountain core which came under threat, including Nant Ffrancon itself. Norman Birkett K.C., a native of Ulverston in the Lake District, and a nonconformist, who chaired the Standing Committee until he became a judge, and who saved Ullswater from desecration, was an inspiration to us all. No wonder that the first legal tome which I bought of my own volition was an annotated volume of the National Parks and Access to the Countryside Act, 1949. In my first real job in local government, with the Lancashire County Council, I was delighted to find that Lancashire still extended to the Lake District, that CPRE had a branch office in County Hall, and that one of my duties was to liaise with the Reverend H.H. Symonds, then Chairman of the Friends of the Lake District: he too had been a member of the Standing Committee, representing the Youth Hostels Association—of which I too was a member.

That is the background which eventually took me to Pembrokeshire at a time when both the County Planning Committee and the National Park Committee were served by the same administration, the latter under the chairmanship of Alderman W.J. Philipps-Williams, the Fishguard solicitor whose breadth of sympathy and eye for landscape made him a better conservator than any appointed member. I did not question the National Park system while I served Pembrokeshire. Doubt set in when I began to see the picture as a whole as an adviser to the Association of County Councils National Parks Committee, which included representatives of all the Parks. This role involved me in negotiations with government departments and the Countryside Commission, and visits to National Park Conferences in various parts of England as well as Wales. Neither did it help to hear certain nominated members of the Snowdonia Committee pontificating, while the first post-1974 Chairman, a formidable Labour member from Llanberis, muttered under his breath (I translate) 'what right has she/he to speak about this? who elected her/him? who does she/he represent?' Almost to the end, however, it was as if I had been programmed by my mother—obtaining funds from the Commission to purchase Ynys Llanddwyn, advising against a Welsh Water scheme at the Bethesda end of Nant Ffrancon (without support from either my National Park colleagues or the National Park Society) or helping to arrange access to the Aran. When someone called Gwynedd a National Park with a County, rather than the other way round, it was not entirely in jest. After some thirty years professional experience of National Parks *in their administrative context*, however, I nevertheless have to concede, not only that the English and Welsh version may have outlived its usefulness everywhere, but that in Wales National Parks have never been well adapted either to the geography or the ethos, and are apt on occasion to be a positive liability. I have come to feel this, not simply as a public servant, but as one of the fauna of the Snowdonia National Park—as someone born and brought up at Dolgellau, under the profound influence of the landscape, as someone who brought up a young family on the edge of the Pembrokeshire National Park, and who has lived ever since within three fields of the Snowdonia boundary, in a locality dominated by the Carneddau. Children and grandchildren of mine are also amongst the fauna of the National Park and likely to remain so.

The phrase about fauna belongs to Clough Williams-Ellis. As Chairman of CPRW, he too was a member of the old Standing Committee on National Parks. Indeed his writings and influence should have secured his beatification by the National Parks lobby at least to the same degree as John Dower, the Committee's Drafting Secretary. Ironically, the Committee was a joint product of both CPRE and CPRW. They acknowledged that Scotland, in some respects, presented a different problem and called for different treatment. (There are no Scottish National Parks: the question was discussed again in depth in 1990-92 but the Scottish Office decided to rely on other methods of conservation). In 1938, only four of the 32 Standing Committee members were Welsh, while CPRW was even less representative of Wales than it is now: somewhat illogically, this Welsh association joined the England-and-Wales conservation and recreation bodies in opposing the creation of a Welsh Countryside Council: perhaps Merfyn Williams's recent appointment as Director promises a change of outlook. But in the thirties, as a result of the Depression, Wales was probably at her lowest civic ebb ever: in 1932, 42% of her insured male population was out of work, while almost 400,000 people left Wales between 1925 and 1939. Today, with Wales so much more self-conscious in every field, and more rigorously studied, it is time to consider the future of the Welsh landscape for ourselves, instead of relying on an essentially English compromise. Before analysing what is wrong and how it could be put right, let me elaborate on my own experience of the present system.

BREAD BEFORE BEAUTY

In my home town, Dolgellau, the designation of Eryri, together with most of Meirionnydd, as the Snowdonia National Park, in 1951, seemed to be generally accepted as a compliment, and a promise of special care. Not long afterwards, however, trade unionists were marching in protest against conservationist opposition to hydro-electricity schemes in the Park, under banners inscribed 'Bread Before Beauty.' In spite of the fact that Plaid Cymru—inspired by the Tennessee Valley Authority created by Roosevelt's New Deal—wished to regenerate the rural economy by using the Welsh power surplus to provide cheap electricity, in Gwynedd it took the party years to live down Labour criticism of its opposition to certain particularly destructive schemes. The growth of disillusion in the quarrying communities can be well understood. After admitting that their unemployment rate was above the average even for Development Areas, Harold Wilson at the Board of Trade had declined to designate them as such: according to his White Paper, 'the numbers involved (were) not significant in the national total.' The working people of the National Park could not have had a more honest illustration of the basic weakness of 'national' policy. On the one hand, the scenery was so important 'nationally' that development was to be inhibited by the designation of a National Park; on the other, the suffering of the people was too insignificant to qualify them for regional aid. Subsequent Labour governments had a better record on regional policy in Gwynedd but, in the 'eighties, the County Council had to fight much the same battle over job losses with the Conservative Welsh Secretary Nicholas Edwards (Lord Crickhowell). As compared with most of Anglesey, the unemployment figures of the quarrying areas have never been fully reflected in their development status.

In 1986, having been invited to speak about economic development to the first annual National Parks Workshop run by the Countryside Commission, I argued that, almost by definition, National Parks are disadvantaged peripheral areas and that, wherever incompatible development was subject to statutory constraints in the 'national' interest, there should be a corresponding 'national' statutory duty to promote compatible development. In a sense, this was implicit in the Sandford Report of 1974 and the Uplands Report of 1984, while a report commissioned from an Edinburgh University research team, *The Economy of Rural Communities in the National Parks of England and Wales* (1981), had recommended that 'the promotion of socio-economic welfare' should become 'a third statutory objective for National Parks.' At the time of my address, Gwynedd, over 55% of which is National Park, with another 10% statutory AONB (Area of Outstanding Natural Beauty) had an unemployment rate of 19.3%, while the rate around Tenby, in South Pembrokeshire, was 36%. Even more to the point, the population of the

Snowdonia National Park had declined 17% between 1951 and 1971—5,000 people in twenty years. Since then, the figure had stabilized as the emigration of the young was masked by an influx of retired people and long-range commuters but in 1983 there had been only three births for every four deaths in the National Park. Crucially, the average income per head was—and still is—particularly low in rural Wales, with average male earnings £13 per week lower than in Wales as a whole in 1984, and £22 lower than in the United Kingdom, to say nothing of the high cost of transport and consumer goods, and the effect of essentially unfair outside competition on the cost of housing. By 1994, almost 40% of the Welsh work-force was still earning less than £212 a week, the highest proportion in any British 'region' to fall below the European Union decency threshold. According to the Department of Employment survey for 1992, the average level in Dyfed, Gwynedd and Powys was between 77% and 84% of the British average, with a greater level of absolute deprivation amongst the lowest 10% of males. Despite a slight boost after the 1992 devaluation, farm income, output and jobs, the foundation of the rural economy, are still in decline, as is the number of farms. It is seldom possible for young people to enter farming without inheriting property: confusion and uncertainty cloud every prospect.

All this was, of course, reflected in the attitude of many councillors. While the National Park was at pains to demonstrate that its development control was no stricter than that of Dwyfor District Council, and creating jobs was difficult in every area remote from a motorway, the fact remained that National Park status was continually being invoked to justify the refusal of planning permission. It was far from easy for National Park Committee members to reject applications with unemployed, or potentially unemployed, people on the public benches, no alternative jobs and vivid press coverage of District Council disagreement with Park policies. 'We have had two conferences on trying to attract more jobs to this area and when there is a chance, the National Park is working against us,' a District Councillor alleges in a *Cambrian News* report—the committee had just refused permission for an extension to the Gwynfynydd gold mine (with several of its small work-force sitting at the back) for a chalet park and for a touring caravan park, all in Meirionnydd, a District so little of which remains outside the Park that it has no planning department of its own.

Well beyond the 'eighties, the classic example of the dilemma facing anyone concerned about both conservation and the local community was the future of the Trawsfynydd Nuclear Power Station. The very presence of such a brutal edifice and line of pylons in a newly designated National Park testifies to the strength of the employment lobby in the 'fifties, though the ancient tag

'Trawsfynydd, hen le hyll
Dynion cam yn torri cyll'

does suggest that, for all its connections with the Romans and with Blodeuwedd, the immediate locality is not one of the highlights of Snowdonia. At the time of the public inquiry, radiation was not the issue. By the eighties, especially after the Chernobyl disaster, which directly blighted dozens of Gwynedd sheep-farms, radiation dominated discussion. The debate over building a successor to the present station, which came to the end of its life in 1994, split the community at first. Under the headline FIGHT IS ON TO SAVE 1,000 JOBS AT TRAWS, the *Cambrian News* reported in 1985, 'Speaker after speaker representing local councils, trade unions and other bodies emphasised that the loss of 600 jobs at the power station and a further 360 jobs indirectly would be a blow from which the area could not recover.' And these were good jobs, many of them good enough to attract well-qualified scientists and technicians back home to an area where employment in the quarries had drastically declined and there was no alternative. In these circumstances, many local people uneasy about nuclear power were prepared to take a chance on Trawsfynydd. At the same time, conservationists with no objection to nuclear power passionately opposed the immense cooling-towers or extended artifical lake which

Trawsfynydd II would have required. Eventually, however, fear of radiation spread from the farming community to villages and towns over a wide area, and seemed to prevail amongst young mothers in particular.

Now that the Government has decided against a second station, it is as well to recall that the County Council and other local authorities, anticipating that no government would consider Trawsfynydd II feasible, began to campaign for alternative employment early in the 'eighties. To the Secretary of State's reluctance to move until a decision about the power-station had actually been taken, they replied that, even with the station operating, the economic prospects of the area were dire. Against the Government's—and the Countryside Commission's—reluctance to accept a duty to promote *compatible* development in a National Park, they argued that no change in legislation was required for a special allocation of funds to the WDA and Mid Wales Development. When the County Council approached the CEGB with a view to setting up a body similar to British Steel Enterprises Ltd. (which had considerable success in replacing jobs lost in the steel industry) they were told that, because of the imminence of privatisation, this would have to be referred to their successors, when established. There was no response to a suggestion that the institution of a National Parks Enterprises Ltd. would be just as appropriate, or that the Trawsfynydd workforce might provide the core of a government research station: only one of about sixty such stations was in Wales, and that—the Welsh Plant Breeding Station at Gogerddan—was in jeopardy. Just outside the National Park, however, a private mineral research firm, Robertson Research of Llandudno, was not only providing over 500 worth-while jobs locally but operating all over the world. (It won the Welsh National Business Award for 1985, beating Laura Ashley, another locally founded firm in rural Wales, into second place.) Some ten years too late, a comparatively modest injection of Welsh Office funds has now commenced but the situation remains desperate. Recently, after public meetings, Blaenau Ffestiniog invited the Home Office to establish a prison in the area: the area was deemed too remote and the prison's 500 jobs will go to Bridgend.

Even if they are not actually within National Parks as such, the example of firms like Robertson and Laura Ashley suggest that there are many Park locations where jobs can be provided on a significant scale. Unfortunately, in an age when image is everything, that is not how foot-loose industry or officialdom as a whole regard the matter. Once, as Chief Executive of the County Council, I had an opportunity to complain privately to one of the less ideological Secretaries of State that the Government was neglecting the Gwynedd economy. He went one better than the usual official response (that £umpteen million were being spent on the A55, 'the road to opportunity'): early the following morning, his private secretary telephoned to ask whether the Council could find a site for a multi-national already considering several areas of the United KIngdom. Within an hour, the firm's list of minimum requirements was duly faxed to me and the Economic Development Officer arrived in my office with a smile on his face and a list of sites. Our euphoria did not last long. The firm's first requirement was that the site should not be in or near a National Park, an AONB, Heritage Coast, a nature reserve or any other protected site. Having ruled out virtually the whole of Gwynedd in that way—we even had 47 town conservation areas—the firm then stipulated that at no time should the site be liable to disturbance by low-flying aircraft... Needless to say, we did our best to suggest that the proximity of protected areas seldom posed problems and were often an advantage in attracting key-workers but it was the last we heard of that particular firm. The main economic drawback of National Park status does not relate to officer recommendation or committee refusal to permit development on particular sites—though this can happen, not always with justification. It relates to the way in which sites in National Parks seldom come into the reckoning: entrepreneurs want as little planning hassle as possible, think in stereotypes and only look at large-scale maps. Government agencies, consultants, even the European Commission, try to fob you off with tourism alone. The very title which evokes warmth amongst holidaymakers, naturalists, ramblers, retired people and estate agents indicates No Go Area to industrialists. One cannot blame them for taking Parliament at its word. Moreover, except sometimes for speculative high-class housing, economic development is the last thing which some influential people wish to see in Gwynedd, not only as individuals with beautiful back-yards—second back-yards some of them—but as Conservatives whose few electoral successes in northern Wales depend on the retirement industry.

CHWAREL Y RHOSYDD

By now, the debate over 'something to replace Trawsfynydd' has moved a little further north and assumed a different form. In 1994, a small local entrepreneur, anticipating the exhaustion of his present quarry, applied for planning permission to reopen the Rhosydd slate mine, 1,800 feet up in the vicinity of Moelwyn Mawr, together with the improvement of the old approach road through Cwm Orthin. When the National Park was designated, Blaenau Ffestiniog and its quarries—strictly speaking, slate-mines—was substantially excluded. In terms of organic planning, this made little sense. It made even less sense that, in drawing the new boundary on the map, the disused Rhosydd quarry was not completely excluded from the Park. In fact, the boundary straddles the Rhosydd complex, including the vast, deep and dangerous pit which contains the working faces. As a result, virtually all the relevant conservation societies sprang into life— the term National Park is more than evocative in these circles, the reaction it prompts is Pavlovian. While the Meirionnydd branch of CPRW decided, significantly, not to oppose the application, their national executive purported to overrule them and joined several other important societies in a direct appeal to the Secretary of State to call the application in. The Secretary of State declined to do so and the County Council, who have jurisdiction over minerals and cross-border applications, have now granted permission, subject to stringent conditions. The Council has the support of the Snowdonia National Park

Committee but both bodies acted against the advice of their planning officers, as well as of the Welsh Countryside Council.

As it happens, the walk up Cwm Orthin to the quarries, and over to Llyn yr Adar and Nant Gwynant, or up Cnicht or Moelwyn Mawr, or directly down the tramway to Croesor, is one which I greatly cherish: there could be no question of granting permission for anything on the untouched ridges, or by the myriad immaculate lakes, to the north. Having read the reports and objections placed before the relevant Planning Sub-committee, one can also appreciate the outstanding interest of the area to industrial archaeologists and CADW. But the reopening of the quarry, and the passing of a few lorry-loads a day down Cwm Orthin, should not deter anyone from crossing the fascinating passes over the plateau: modern methods do not produce as much spoil as the old quarries and the slate will be processed elsewhere. Cwm Orthin was still a workplace when Wyn Griffith crossed over to Nant Gwynant as a boy: when he wrote about this so lyrically in his prime, he did not even mention the quarries: 'a cloud of boredom and even of dislike… evaporated in the thin air above fifteen hundred feet and a sense of joy and exhilaration took its place.' Decades later, the young poet Gwyn Thomas could only see in Cwm Orthin (in translation)

> 'Iron wheels, their teeth rusty, on their backs
> Like terrible old mouths, old jaws of whales;
> Old eyeless ruins, like empty skulls…'

and 'emptiness, emptiness, emptiness.' In his fine essay on Moelwyn Mawr, it is on the oppression of the big Victorian quarryowner-landlords that Jim Perrin meditates, on the 200 men who lived in the Rhosydd quarry barracks under slum conditions, on the average age of decease of 37 for slate-miners, and 67 for other men, at Blaenau in 1875: 'There are times when, thinking of these things, I cannot bear to pick my way through the dereliction of Rhosydd…'

From the purely selfish view of an occasional visitor, I should probably prefer Moelwyn Mawr and its surroundings to be left as

20

I have always known them. What I cannot understand is the sense of outrage with which the conservation societies, including individuals whom I respect, oppose the safeguarding and possible creation of a significant number of jobs, in the traditional industry of the district, in an environment already dominated by the eerie ruins of that industry, *at a time of economic crisis when nothing else palpable whatsoever is on offer* to enable Blaenau Ffestiniog to survive as a community: as for conservation, ought not the conservation of one of the few substantial communities in which Welsh is the dominant language have precedence over the conservation of the two pairs of choughs about which the RSPB expressed concern? It is not that the prospects for Rhosydd are rosy, the jobs without risk or the reopened quarries in any way sufficient as an economic base for the locality. It is the utter failure of the central authorities, or of the entrepreneurs who must exist in the ranks of the large conservation societies, to offer Blaenau Ffestiniog any alternative which is appalling. How can the Countryside Council be so academic as to conclude their objection, 'CCW also has a duty to have regard to the economic and social needs of rural Wales... In this context, the approved Gwynedd Structure Plan is clear that employment provision in this area is concentrated on employment estates at Blaenau Ffestiniog and Penrhyndeudraeth.' Structure Plans tend inevitably to relate to a static world: who could have foreseen in 1953, or even in 1993, that a modest revival in the slate industry might involve the Rhosydd? For that matter, is not the replacement of the lost 'national' nuclear power jobs a 'national' matter?

CONSERVATION BY CONSENT

The ideal solution to the Rhosydd dilemma would probably be to buy out the quarry on terms which neither the owner, the quarrymen nor the community could refuse. There is a precedent of sorts in agricultural set-aside, though the local community around Ffestiniog needs the opportunity to be more active, rather than less. Normally, in the United Kingdom, an arrogant and inflated centre dictates its own terms; in the case of Rhosydd, a maverick Secretary of State seems, for once, to have allowed the County Council to play its own card. The situation is reminiscent of several cases in Graubünden (Il Grischun in Romansch) where, in considering hydro-electric schemes, local communes usually put their own interests before those of either the federal conservation lobby or the power industry. Graubünden is the Swiss canton in which the communes have retained most authority: permission to dam an upland valley and licence the use of water power is a matter for them, though companies have a limited right of quasi-judicial appeal to the cantonal, and then the federal government, where a minority of communes is, without 'sufficient' or 'substantial' grounds, holding up a scheme involving several. Such is the power of a Bündner commune, and the respect accorded to all communes in the political culture of Switzerland, that Segl (Sils) in the Upper Engadine has twice been compensated—substantially by voluntary subscription— first for refusing permission for the inclusion of the incomparable Lej da Segl (Silsersee) in a hydro-electricity scheme, secondly, in 1980, for revoking a local plan which had (somewhat inadvert- ently, at a time of little pressure for second homes) zoned land at the eastern end of the lake for housing. With a different object, Splügen and Medels successfully managed, almost single-handed, to defy tremendous pressure (accompanied by generous compen- sation) from the federal and cantonal governments and the industrial lobby to allow the drowning of much of the upper Hinterrhein valley, including most of the main village. This occurred during the second World War, when Switzerland was isolated and the military high command considered it essential to reduce dependence on imported electricity, coal and oil. The contrast with the unsuccessful campaign against drowning Capel Celyn in Cwm Tryweryn in 1957 could not be more striking. In spite of the offer of a slightly more expensive alternative, Liverpool Corporation had little difficulty in defeating the unanimous residents, the district and county councils, the Welsh local authorities as a whole, and all the Welsh M.P.s but two. From the point of view of justice and the rule of law, there could not be a better illustration of the superiority of a written constitution over unlimited parliamentary sovereignty. Yet it was Capel Celyn which lay within a National Park, while the Ramblers' Association declined to object to the drowning.

It is perhaps a recent Swiss case which is the most instructive of all, the case of the Greina, one of the high uninhabited sources of the Vorderrhein, whose remote beauty is matched by the unique interest of its flora and geology. If there were National Parks on the English model in Switzerland, the Greina would have been the inner sanctuary of one of the finest. The federal conservation societies were determined to save it from the electricty companies. When the Swiss nuclear power programme was postponed in deference to public apprehension, however, the industrial lobby was just as determined to secure more hydro-electric power. Everything rested on three small communes, and on Vrin and Somvitg (Somvix) in particular. There could be no appeal against a decision on their part to allow the scheme to go ahead; unlike neighbouring communes with such schemes, they had never managed to obtain licence fees, royalties and free electricity allocations to reduce their rates and improve their schools and services; and they were disposed to grant permission. Eventually, however, the federal government intervened and made an unprecedented offer of compensation to the communes, sufficient for them to feel that they had eaten their cake and kept it. At the same time, the government announced that their next bill on water resources would include provision whereby any commune could be compensated for declining to permit a scheme on conservationist grounds. What struck me about the scheme's opponents was their tendency to accept the principle that small communes are entitled to make the best of local resources: opposition was mainly directed at the prosperous parts of Switzerland and at the federal government, rather than the local people, many of whom were able to sing a specially composed Romansch defence song, *Il Clom della Greina* (The Call of the Greina), with a clear social conscience. This too is in marked and pleasant contrast to the opposition mounted to the Rhosydd scheme. Throughout decades of depopulation, unemployment and low wages, the well-heeled opposition to development in rural Wales has usually been entirely negative in its approach to economic problems more severe than those of rural Graubünden. It also looks as if the Swiss method of bargaining and buying out is the more effective. Here, central authority extends its dominion, keeps down its costs and disarms weak-kneed opponents beneath a cloak of high sentiment. There, Swiss mutualism cuts out hypocrisy and accepts the underlying issue as one of finance, rather than standards.

Negotiation is preferable to force in designating protected areas as well as in settling particular issues. In a recent study, Jane Carruthers complains that the prelude to the South African National Parks Act of 1926 is usually presented as 'a contest between the forces of "good" (those in favour of national parks) and "evil" (those antagonistic or apathetic to the idea).' The creation of the Kruger National Park was indeed draconian in its impact upon black hunters, if not white farmers, but national parks proper in undeveloped regions seldom impinge upon substantial populations and complex economies like the milder regimes of England and Wales. In Wales, some 80,000 people live within national park boundaries, while the parks themselves form part of the hinterland of more densely populated areas. Here too one can agree with Carruthers that 'fundamentally, the founding of a national park... is a political, social and economic issue more than a moral one.' 'Whose heritage?' asks Terence Ranger, the doyen of Zimbabwe historians, in the title of an article on the Matobo National Park, in the hills known by whites as 'the Matopos', hills as singular for religious and political inlays as for soaring and bulbous outcrops. This too is a question which has not always been properly addressed in Wales.

CONSERVATION BY COMMAND

The legislation which authorized the designation of National Parks was part of the great Labour programme of 1945 which also gave us Aneurin Bevan's National Health Service, Jim

Griffiths's National Insurance and a number of nationalized industries, including a notably successful electricity industry. It seems nevertheless to have been the local Labour movement in Gwynedd which first became alarmed by the possible consequences of creating National Park Boards; then the Welsh County Councils took the lead in ensuring that, after the creation of Boards for the English Lake District and the Peak, the next seven National Parks were administered by county council committees or, as in the Brecon Beacons today, joint committees. The proportion of members nominated by the government, one-third of the total, remained the same on the committees, however, and the difference between a Committee and a Board became almost negligible after the reorganization of 1974. County Councils are obliged by statute to delegate all national park functions to the National Park Committee. These include the planning functions which, outside a National Park, are administered by the Borough or District Council. As a matter of law, each Committee is obliged to appoint a National Park Officer to head a separate department. While National Park Boards can formally precept upon County Councils in the same way as a Police Authority (that is, demand funds as of right), in practice the Committees too have been financed in the same way since 1974, with three quarters of the expenditure being met centrally, and a quarter locally, in each Park: this is to continue if, as the Government propose in the Environment Bill, all the Parks are administered by Boards. In the House of Lords, Lord (Dafydd) Elis-Thomas went out of his way to allege that the 25% was not always forthcoming from the Gwynedd County Council, amongst others, 'when it should have been': as it happens, however unhappy councillors may have been to see the government increasing, not so much national park expenditure, as the expected (non-statutory) local contribution, in a general situation of severe cuts, substantially the Gwynedd contribution only fell short in 1993-94 when (after giving 12 months notice) the Council failed to repeat an increase of no less than 34.5% provided in the previous year; at the time, other services were yet again being cut back, by as much as £2m. in the case of education. In spite of this, over the five years beginning in 1991-92, the expenditure of the Snowdonia National Park will nevertheless have risen from £2.132m. to some £3.1m. and a new purpose built headquarters will have been provided for it in the centre of the Park. In strict law, county councils could always have extended their cuts to their own share of National Park expenditure: in practice, dependent as they too were upon government grant, the most a Council could risk was an occasional show of reluctance. Local government finance is notoriously complicated: even if there was more substance in Lord Elis-Thomas's point, however, the Welsh County Councils might—at a time of acute Thatcherism—have expected sympathy rather than indignation on the part of the National Park lobby as a whole, let alone a former Gwynedd M.P.. In the circumstances, their frequent praise for the Peak National Park Board might also have been put in perspective. The Board is supported by local authorities with a population of 8 million, as opposed to the 220,000 who support Snowdonia: when local resources were measured in terms of rateable value, the combined rateable value per head of the former was £20 per head higher than that of Gwynedd. In 1983/84, the Peak Board's precept added a rate of 0.07p. to that of its constituent authorities, while Gwynedd had to levy over a penny for Snowdonia, a penny which would, on occasion, have obviated the need for cuts in, say, the social services: yet in 1974, before the economic crisis hit government spending, the Director of the Countryside Commission had personally assured Gwynedd that the allocation of National Park Grant would take into account both the outstanding importance of Snowdonia and the limited resources of the County Council. As the example of most Police Authorities suggests, the change from informal convention to statutory precept is unlikely to be more than academic.

Normally, a National Park Committee's resolutions are submitted to the full Council for information only. From the point of view of local democracy, the sole advantage of a committee rather than a board is that the former is subject to the general administrative controls which apply to all county committees in such spheres as finance, personnel and billingualism:

in the fields delegated to it by statute, a county council cannot tell a National Park Committee to change its policies, priorities or staffing structure: on the advice of the County Treasurer or Personnel Officer, it might have something to say about a lax procedure unearthed by the internal auditor or the grading of a National Park post in comparison with similar jobs elsewhere. Here again, however, Boards too are often advised by county chief officers, or were so before the government's insistence on competitive tendering and internal markets. Somebody has to do this work in the interests of good housekeeping. If the County Councils lose the role, the Countryside Council or the Welsh Office will fill the gap and, as the Colleges of Further Education are finding, 'independence' will merely expose the National Parks to remoter devils they do not know. The National Park lobby has nevertheless shed gallons of crocodile tears about unsympathetic county councils: seldom indeed has anything more significant been at stake than the *amour propre* of a National Park Officer or Chairman. Every Council committee sheds similar tears from time to time. The only difference in the case of National Park Officers—and some members—is that they have been encouraged to regard themselves as part of a 'national' service and that, for most of them, the enhancement of this national role is the surest avenue of advance.

To be lectured by the County Treasurer or coaxed by the County Personnel Officer is a condition endemic to local government: Chief Executives themselves put up with it: at a time of retrenchment, it is usually salutary. One regrets that a similar service appeared to be lacking in central government when no less than £1.5 billion was wasted on setting up, administering and replacing the Poll Tax, over £1 billion of which is likely to remain uncollected—to say nothing of the 4d. in the £ which could have been taken off this year's income tax if the Poll Tax had been killed off by good, sceptical advice at the start, instead of being facilitated by an insular Environment Department isolated both from other European systems and English local authorities. Significantly, Sir William Kerr Fraser, permanent secretary at the Scottish Office until 1988, strongly cautioned his ministers against the tax. (See Butler, Adonis and Travers, *Failure in British Government,* Oxford University Press, 1994, p.180, 206-223, 275).

It is nevertheless difficult to blame individual National Park officers for concluding, during the past decade or so, that local government was a sinking ship and that the national park offered a lifeline from the point of view of resources and respect. For its part, an ambitious Countryside Commission saw the appointment of statutory National Park Officers as a key element in bringing the Parks under their direct influence and control. Promoting the idea of a 'family of national parks' at interesting conferences and workshops, pressing induction courses upon national park members, basing the payment of grant on detailed plans drawn up in conjunction with their own staff, the Commission took the sting out of a National Park's increasing dependence on their goodwill by skilfully inflating the sense of mission and self-importance of their officers, as well as of some councillors who had managed to carve out a surer fiefdom within a National Park. The Commission also made the most of a legitimate point: that hill farmers should look to the conservation purse for compensation for the loss of production grants. Some of their supporters falsely claimed that Boards would be able to oblige reluctant councils to hand over to the National Parks additional funds for farming. Some farmers' leaders deemed it prudent to keep the goodwill of a possible source of further income: to the consternation of many of its members, even the FUW appeared to make a U-turn and express support for Lord Norrie's Bill.

From Whitehall's point of view, the Commission's original job was to act as a buffer between the militants of the countryside lobby and the public purse. As the lobby grew more vociferous, and green votes began to count, it became necessary to yield rather more. Again, the founding of the Council of National Parks as an umbrella for some forty leading conservation societies, and the inclusion of national park representatives upon it, made the lobby more coherent and less raw. Few realize that the core funding of the Council of National Parks and many of its member societies is met by the taxpayer: this even applies to the Snowdonia National Park Society, established because the Caernarvonshire

28

Branch of CPRW, respected and effective in practice, lacked the stridency beloved of militants. (The Society declined a formal request to change its name: for many years, its counter-productive style harmed the image of the National Park Committee.) In 1991, the Commission claimed that the CNP represented voluntary societies with a combined membership of 3.4 million: no figure was given for Wales and no allowance made for the fact that many people belong to several organisations whose aims sometimes conflict. The officers and committees of such societies tend to be more single-minded than the membership as a whole. Neither is the membership consulted frequently on particular issues. As an ordinary member, I have myself been included thrice over in a total said to be opposed to something which I support. Some CNP leaders have no compunction about threatening county councillors that tens of millions of urban electors will insist on overriding them: such is their concept of democracy.

THE HIDDEN AGENDA

If some conservation societies are much less representative than they claim, however, the increasing tendency for conurbation dwellers with only a superficial knowledge of the countryside to give them tacit support could give more significance to the rather formal distinction between a national park committee and a national park board. If the change from committee to board was the end of the matter, there would be little point in promoting boards except to create an illusion of influence and progress ('clarity of vision and self-confidence' as the Review Panel put it.) But the Government itself may now have a hidden agenda for the national parks: it is certainly not enamoured of elected councillors: councillors have been excluded from Health Authorities and their number drastically reduced on the governing bodies of colleges of further education. Between 1965 and 1985, the proportion of councils controlled by a political party or coalition increased from 50% to 84%. At the same time, the Tories were becoming weaker and weaker in local government: according to the scholarly authors of *Failure in British Government*, this bred 'fierce resentment' amongst the Tory élite. While two National Park Boards amongst ten were comparatively safe from becoming full-blown quangos, a whole system of Boards could well be eased out of local democracy altogether. There can be no doubt that the countryside lobby has its sights on that: at a time when the standing of local government was high, the Hobhouse Committee, which paved the way for the 1949 Act, recommended that only 50% of the members should be elected. In 1965, the Standing Committee pressed for legislative changes in the light of fifteen years experience of this act: these included the appointment by the Minister of the Chairman in addition to 'not less than half' of the members. This too was the proportion 'most frequently suggested' in evidence to the National Parks Review Panel as recently as 1991. However limited the Environment Bill may be in its immediate effect, however moderate the ministers, however reassuring the CNP leaders, the more militant agenda is barely hidden. The voluntary societies felt betrayed when the 1949 Act failed to produce universal boards. Every subsequent change has stemmed from their conviction that their beloved National Parks are unsafe in the hands of the inhabitants and their represent-atives. As for the Countryside Commission, they too are burdened by the civilizing mission of the less avaricious type of empire builder. 'Over my dead body,' said a leading Commissioner when I first broached the idea of a Welsh equivalent separate from Cheltenham. When had I last heard that phrase? Were they not the words of a distinguished English mountaineer, by then a formidable Establishment man with the low profile that used to go with high power: 'over my dead body,' was his remark when, after the establishment of a Welsh Sports Council, it was assumed that Plasybrenin, the mountain centre at Capel Curig, would come under its wing: to this day, it remains under *The* Sports Council. On the whole, however, the National Park movement is more of a church than an empire. It used to include leaders like evangelists. It may produce successors more in the mould of the animal rights movement.

Not that most National Park Board enthusiasts are, as it were, acting locally to conserve the globe. However worthy their motives, ramblers and bird-watchers as such should not assume the righteous indignation proper to attacking the First World's disproportionate contribution to the Greenhouse Effect, and to defending the 1500 hungry children who die *every hour* in the Third World.

The combination of a Commission bent on extending its bureaucratic empire, of local agents with better prospects within—rather than without—that empire, of voluntary movements with an uncompromising sense of mission, and of a brand name as evocative as National Park, was difficult to resist. Even before local democracy reached its lowest ebb after a decade of Thatcherism, the Association of County Councils was far from single-minded about maintaining local control of National Parks: only three of the eight Welsh Counties have a major stake in them, while several English Parks are politically insignificant in relation to their own local authorities—which is natural enough if a National Park is indeed 'wilderness.' Any dispute between the ACC and the Commission tended to be a phoney war which drew attention away from the real issues of conserving the countryside. In 1989, ostensibly to celebrate forty years of National Parks, the Commission set up the National Parks Review Panel to assess how 'national park purposes' might be most effectively achieved in the future. Their report, published in January 1991, is the basis for the proposals in the Environment Bill whereby all Parks will be run by Boards. (Lord Norrie's private Bill was talked out last year, first by Plaid Cymru and then by Michael Jopling, a former Agriculture Minister with constituency interests in both the Lake District and the Yorkshire Dales.) While the report is a useful summary of conventional thought on the developing pressures upon National Parks, it displays little of the creative agony of the Sandford Report of 1976 ('people have begun to destroy what they have come to enjoy'). Some recommendations, such as that on 'real income support in recognition of the difficulties of farming in the national parks and the tasks performed in the public interest' are admirable. Generally speaking, however, the Panel evaded the problems. In spite of the fact that a separate Welsh Countryside Council was about to be established—probably through the prescience of Sir Richard Lloyd Jones at the Welsh Office—the report has nothing to say about Wales. In spite of having had John Toothill, the Lake District National Park Officer, as a member, it fails to reflect the crisis which prompted his despairing Board to promote a radical, if abortive, private parliamentary bill as the only hope of saving community and landscape from external pressures, such as the pricing of local people out of the housing market: to have recognised the despair of so many Cumbrians would have meant discussing not only positive discrimination in favour of local people but tourist taxes and restricting access for ecological reasons—as happens in United States National Parks with the support of users such as the Sierra Club. No attempt was made to compare the performance of, respectively, Boards, Committees and Districts Councils with AONBs in key areas such as development control; or to consider how development control could be made more objective, and adopting plans more deeply democratic. On the question of Boards, the Panel was innocent of any thought on constitutional propriety or political science, a common failing in a culture which confuses civics with Public Relations. Its outlook was too bland to address the paradox that conservation management itself suburbanises the country, 'the irony of victory,' as Roderick Nash puts it: 'that the necessary means defeat the desired end.'

Apart from the Chairman (who is certainly as Welsh as Vinnie Jones) there was only one Welsh member of the Review Panel of 13—of the ten Parks designated in the 'fifties, three were in Wales, but 288 sq. km. of the Broads was added in 1988. (Snowdonia has 2,171 sq.km.) This may have seemed generous in terms of the relative populations of Wales and England: in terms of important landscape, however, Wales is—within Britain—a big power and should act like one. But the Welsh statesmen who talk loudest about the virtues of business have a blind spot when it comes to bargaining on behalf of their own country: they give away their best cards; they seldom realize that, when London talks about widening horizons, the object is, all too often, something for nothing. As soon as the membership of the Panel was announced, the ACC knew that a recommendation to create Boards was inevitable. The Director of the Commission was both a member of the Panel and its assessor. Evidence in confidence was invited and county councils given no details of statements accepted to the effect that the link with County Councils unduly 'constrained' National Park Committees and deflected them from their purposes. If anything, the reverse was the case. This aspect of the matter has deceived those who rely on official reports and lack *intimate* experience of the matters in question: it is tempting to elaborate, as well as to demonstrate the persistent disregard for previous assurance which characterised relations between the Commission and local government between, to my own knowledge, the run-up to the 1972 Act and the holding of the Review. This was facilitated by the fact that, between 1979 and 1994, the average tenure of an Environment Secretary was only 1.6 years, while on National Park matters the Welsh Office appeared to be playing second fiddle to the Bristol office of the Environment Department. For over twenty years, scant opportunity was ever given to county councils to put their case on the National Parks to government, let alone see, challenge and cross-examine any case against them. Yet, in Gwynedd, during the years when County Councils had the right to call in planning decisions which contravened the Structure Plan, the County Planning Committee appeared to be just as dedicated to conservation as the National Park Committee. All planners give the utmost weight to statutory landscape designations and county planning officers tend to be—if only because their salaries reflect larger territories and more varied duties—at least as formidable as their national park equivalents. But it would never do for the Commission to acknowledge that, as often as not, a national park might be in good hands outside their system. As happens frequently in official life, having had their views included in what appears, superficially, to be the report of an independent and representative panel, the Commission and their supporters can now refer to it as impartial authority for what they already wanted to believe.

THE REAL ISSUES

If the reader is beginning to think that the debate over National Parks is primarily the type of inter-service sectarian war to which the English bureaucracy is particularly prone—the kind of dispute in which MI5 derives greater satisfaction from taking a rise out of the Special Branch than from thwarting the KGB—he is close to the truth. Sometimes it is indeed difficult to reconcile the conservation of landscape with making a living; sometimes the 'national' interest in the former is at odds with the local interest in creating jobs; sometimes one can understand why conservationists might prefer to take planning decisions out of the hands of local democracy. In practice, however, the major threats to the landscape come not from local government or local businesses but from central government and large-scale industry—from the armed forces with their training camps, low-flying jets, and grinding helicopters, from national and European agricultural policies, from motorways, from the major electricity and quarrying companies, from major tourist and speculative housing projects which depend on outside labour and offer few local jobs. All this could be deduced from the Review Panel report. Sometimes, as in the case of the Trawsfynydd Power Station, the benefit to the local economy of a centrally run undertaking is overwhelming. Even in a case as clear-cut as Trawsfynydd, however, there would have been little local support for a nuclear power station had there been any alternative. Other things being equal, what local community would not prefer safe, clean and handsome development to any other? How many farming families would not prefer to maintain the way of life which kept their forefathers on the land than resort to overstocking in response to central policy in the era of the supermarket?

The major conservation problem of the United Kingdom is

how to defend the land against *central* government and the major interests upon which Conservative governments in particular tend to depend. But the separate administration established to defend the national parks, now to become even more 'independent' of local (but not central) government, generally comes to bear on such people as family farmers wanting mobile caravan sites or small shopkeepers whose signs are too big, matters which any self-respecting community ought to be able to regulate for itself. Is there any evidence that the record of most National Parks is any better, by and large, or any worse, than most District Councils in this respect—particularly since county councils lost the right to defend their own structure plans? The Welsh Office rejection of the housing section of the Gwynedd County Council Structure Plan, which limited growth to local need, was a significant backward step from the point of view of conservation. The substitution of a National Park Board for a National Park Committee cannot change matters like that or make a whit of difference to the standard of development control.

The phoney choice between national parks and local democracy clouds the issue in a more fundamental way too. The future of the landscape depends, not on special treatment here and there, but on creating a sustainable economy and habitat, and a responsible society, throughout Wales, and in every English region, and giving this matter priority at every level of government. Lacking the day-to-day nagging in public which only a Welsh Parliament can provide, the Welsh Office has not even sorted out the bewildering variety of programmes aimed at reducing harmful agricultural impact upon the rural ecology itself, in a field in which interdependence is everything. This is not the place to expand on the future of rural society generally: the essentials may be explored in the work of a Welsh thinker of international stature, Raymond Williams, who was born and brought up at Pandy, on the edge of the Brecon Beacons National Park. Raymond Williams's criticism of high-input large-scale farming is essentially that of a true—not a week-end—countryman, 'a friend of bracken above a thousand feet and an enemy below that contour.' Rejecting the way in which mainstream socialism apes capitalism in putting production and profit above livelihood—a full life—he aimed for a 'green socialism' in which economics and ecology form 'a single science and source of value, leading on to a new politics of equitable livelihood.' At the same time, he remained a negotiator, not a fundamentalist; a student of specific cases, not a simplifier; a moderniser, not a Utopian like the William Morris whose questioning of mass production he did respect.

All too often, the places we are trying to conserve stand in the way of the main economy. Unless that economy changes, conservation will lose battle after battle, within the National Parks themselves. As Professor Gareth Wyn Jones, the distinguished Deputy Director of the Welsh Countryside Council, pointed out in 1993, even if every relevant state fulfils its international obligations to curb the emissions which cause acid rain, the level of acidity in certain delectable Sites of Special Scientific Interest in the Eryri National Park will still be too high to restore life to the affected lakes. (To think that Pembroke Power Station may be allowed to convert to orimulsion!) Again, as Robert Minhinnick argued in a previous *Changing Wales* essay, tourism— 'now the most important Welsh industry'—'is doing its level best to destroy what many people consider the two essential characteristics of Wales—its environment and its culture.' Yet the need for road improvements in Eryri, even for measures to combat erosion on more and more footpaths, depend in the main, not on the local tourist trade, or on resorts like Llandudno just outside the National Park, but on the attitude of the English conurbations to the question of boosting public transport and curbing the motor car and—at the European level—the mammoth freight vehicle. Substantially, it is the conurbations which are polluting and exploiting the countryside and it is there that 'national park values' have truly to be enforced. To restrict modest Welsh Office trunk road improvements in Eryri as part of a general policy of restricting the size of lorries and the number of urban private cars would be admirable. To restrict road improvements in the National Parks and do little in the conurbations is—as the volume of traffic continues to mount— to discriminate against communities already disadvantaged.

For the Council of National Parks to send out press releases in which Chris Bonington (the Will Carling of English climbing) declares that 'the future of Wales' national parks hangs in the balance unless new legislation to provide better protection for them is brought forward urgently' was meaningless in the context of Lord Norrie's Bill to create Boards. It lacks all sense of proportion in relation to the national park sections of the Environment Bill too. Or does the hidden agenda extend to something on the lines of the United States Wilderness Act of 1964, according to which a wilderness 'generally appears to have been affected primarily by the forces of nature, with the imprint of man's work substantially unnoticeable' and within which 'man himself is a visitor who does not remain'? In spite of everything, this could still apply to about 70% of the Earth, if not to Wales.

When the Cumbrian poet Norman Nicholson ended his essentially conservationist *Portrait of the Lakes* with the words 'A thriving West Cumberland and a prosperous ring of market towns in Westmorland and North Lancashire are essential if the Lakes are to retain anything of independence and dignity. Let industrial Cumberland decay, and the National Park will become no more than a convalescent home for a sick civilization,' he was referring to physical regional planning as well as to sense of community. In any case, sophisticated regional planning does involve what the great American planner Lewis Mumford called 'the inner environment.' Up to a point, the pioneers of the English or Welsh National Park recognized this. Even Wordsworth's well-known appeal to 'persons of pure taste who, by their visits... to the Lakes in the North of England, testify that they deem the district a sort of national property' is usually quoted out of context: in fact, the great poet was appealing for help against an influx of wealthy 'strangers' who were, even then, buying out the local community and substituting their own bad taste for the simplicity of the dales. Pauline Dower considered 'the preservation of the living tradition of rural life (to be) the key to the future of the National Parks.' Clough Williams-Ellis emphasized that he was not advocating 'the sterilization of my native hills,' that 'the more the bracken is kept in its place, which is amongst the

37

boulders, the more frequent the farms… the better,' that 'development of an affectionate and realistic kind will enhance' the beauty of Eryri, that there can be 'many forests, twice as many and twice as good homes… even a few more and better roads.' But the socialism of his day was centralist in spirit. Today both Social and Liberal Democrats stress participation, or what Raymond Williams calls 'conceding the practice of democracy.' It is the Conservatives who have turned their backs on Burke and the traditional English local liberties of which they were once proud. It is the Market which thrusts upon us regional divisions of prosperity as ruthless and uneven as those of any Stalinist social engineer. The characteristic fear of democracy of the English Establishment and civil service retains its hold. Are there still planners in the Department of the Environment like the important figure whom I heard maintaining, at a private meeting in the sixties, that employment should only be promoted in the favoured South East of England, and that the uplands should be reserved for recreation and wildlife? It has certainly been argued in the 'outdoor' press that, in the National Parks, the government should give recreation precedence over subsidized farming. Neither is it reassuring that, according to the 1985 circular, *The Economic Efficiency of National Park Authorities,* the designation of a Park is 'a formal acknowledgement of the outstanding natural beauty of some of Britain's more remote and wild countryside.' London and Cheltenham certainly seem remote from Dolgellau but the mild grey well-built labyrinth of warm-hearted Dolgellau *wild?* Its chapels, church, hotels and banks, seen across the alluvial green of the Marian Mawr, whose cricket pavilion was dated 1826, *wilder* than a veduta of Oxford? Brecon, the source of the first printed volume in Welsh and the home of Europe's largest jazz festival *wild* (in the circular's sense)? Tenby, the home of Gwen John, and of Robert Recorde, author of the first mathematics textbooks in English and inventor of the = sign, *wild?* And Manorbier where, even in the Twelfth Century, there was— according to Giraldus Cambrensis—'plenty of wine for sale'? Or for that matter Llanuwchllyn or Mynachlog-ddu or Myddfai?

Arne Naess, the great Norwegian conservationist, has appealed for modesty in man's relationship, not only with mountains, but with mountain people. He was thinking principally of the Himalaya but his attitude is as relevant to access to the Aran, as to the more vivid problem of protecting Sherpa culture in Nepal. The English Lakes without echoes of Wordsworth's 'perfect Republic of Shepherds and Agriculturists'—and of Nicholson's iron-miners and furnacemen—the Aran without O.M. Edwards's *gwerin,* the peaks of the Engiadina Bassa without the cubist windows, arched entrances, Romansch inscriptions and sgraffiti of F'tan, Guarda and Ardez, the fluted ice walls and inviolate summits of Gang Chenpo without Bhotian Alps and Buddhist sanctuaries: the one without the other is—as I have so often felt and said—in each case unthinkable. One of the gains in the new Environment Bill is that the objects of a National Park are to include conserving and enhancing, not only natural beauty and wildlife as before, but also the 'cultural heritage' of the area. A National Park authority is also to 'have regard to the economic and social well-being of local communities within the National Park.' I like to think of both additions as tributes to the tenacity of the elected members of the Snowdonia National Park Committee. In the face of some criticism, they added the new economic objective to their own objectives at least a decade ago: only last autumn, however, the CNP was implacably opposed to its inclusion in Lord Norrie's Bill. As for culture, the proceedings of the Snowdonia National Park Committee have always been conducted mainly in Welsh, as is only natural. If some are astonished at the emphasis the committee put on the language, let them remember that as cosmopolitan a mountain-walker, and as formidable a scholar, as can be imagined, George Steiner no less, describes 'the destruction of natural linguistic diversity' as 'perhaps the least reparable of the ecological ravages which distinguish our age.' The presence of a distinct language is plain for all to see in Snowdonia, North Pembrokeshire and the Brecon Beacons west of the Storey Arms. The last Welsh-speakers in the Black Mountains died about fifty years ago but the subtler distinguishing marks of the Border Country and of South Pembrokeshire are equally threatened by a lack of economic continuity. So are their civic identities, and that in part because, for planning purposes, they have been deprived of fully democratic local government and subjected to artificial boundaries. Roy Hattersley recently warned the Labour Party of the dangers of 'a political party becoming a philosophy-free zone.' There are dangers in creating administrative units without a sound basis in political science. The National Parks were a typical product of English muddling through at a time when, in a more or less organic society with quiescent fringes, this sort of thing more or less worked. But the communities of the National Parks have civic as well as cultural identities, civic identities not without vivid links with Glyndŵr and Tom Ellis, Rebecca and Waldo Williams, Hywel Harris and Dic Penderyn. They are entitled to the same rights as the rest of us in planning as in everything else. Such rights cannot be extinguished, or bought out, by a payment of grant-aid proportionately greater even than that paid for other local purposes (which now runs at about 90% on average in Wales, though what we receive is, of course, our own taxes recycled at the Treasury in London and then in the Welsh Office.)

According to Mountain Agenda, the international group established to draw the attention of the Earth Summit at Rio to the declining state of the the world's mountains, 'sustainable development can only be meaningfully formulated (in the Alps) if it is designed in the most decentralised manner possible,' with the communes and their citizens and regional groups of communes playing a crucial role. Was there no member of the National Parks Review Panel who could appreciate that point? What central government can legitimately do if it disapproves of a local decision is to negotiate with elected authorities in possession of the same rights as authorities outside the Parks.The self-respect—the political self-respect—of communities in the National Parks is part of what is there to be conserved. They have the right to protect their own heritage. Without apron-strings, they will take a greater pride in that heritage. What a tragedy that the national park lobby, guided partly by single-issue enthusiasts, partly by time-servers, decided long ago to take on local rather than central government. Together, the landscape lobby and local government could have made a greater impact. Even so, the National Park probably had its uses as a prototype for all rural areas. The time has come to apply its lessons to all areas worth conserving, to move beyond National Parks, particularly in Wales.

THE PROBLEM OF BEAUTIFUL WALES

Few of the English National Parks are large and significant in relation to their surrounding counties: psychologically, Devon without Dartmoor is a Gwynedd without the Migneint/Rhobell Fawr block rather than a Gwynedd without the 55% of the county included in the Eryri National Park: with the loss of Anglesey and Aberconwy after reorganization, the proportion in the successor county based on Caernarfon will be about three quarters, much of the rest AONB, ESA or Heritage Coast, not to mention the additional local authority Landscape Conservation Areas which only appear on Local Plans. In Wales as a whole, the proportion of National Park is about 20%: had a Cambrian Mountains National Park been created in central Wales, as formally proposed by the Countryside Commission, and still coveted by the CNP, the proportion would have been nearer 30%: if one adds the other types of protected landscape, over half rural Wales is already covered. In a sense, this is as it should be. Most of Wales is beautiful: now that the Valleys are becoming green again, industrial Wales too lacks the monotonous wastes of the Black Country and South Lancashire and the vast built-up areas of London and the English Midlands. In Wales, the weaknesses of the English National Park concept are nevertheless aggravated in two ways. On the one hand, so great a proportion of Wales is protected that the coinage of designation has already been debased. On the other hand, all over Wales there remains landscape which should, by English standards, have been designated as National Park but which does not qualify for supplementary grant: Pumlumon, for example, or the Twm Siôn

41

Cati country between the heads of Teifi and Tywi, or the Radnor Forest; the Llŷn peninsula or Gower; the Berwyn; Hiraethog, perhaps: Hiraethog certainly if one adds to it the head of Dyffryn Clwyd, Moel Fama, Eglwyseg... Every landscape is unique but these must be the equal of the Northumberland National Park, even without the equivalent of Hadrian's Wall, or the North York Moors, even if those Moors do provide a fine contrast to the featureless Vale of York, and Rievaulx Abbey outranks Valle Crucis: but neither Tintern Abbey nor the wood-wandering stretches of the Wye in which Wordsworth dwelt 'so oft in spirit' are within a National Park as opposed to an AONB.

If so high a proportion of Wales is beautiful that almost any demarcation of National Parks in Wales is invidious, the way in which beautiful landscape is intertwined with the working parts of the economy also detracts from the present National Parks as natural planning regions and communities. The detachment of the Lake District from western Cumbria—Norman Nicholson's point—is surpassed in idiocy by the islanding of Blaenau Ffestiniog in the middle of the Snowdonia National Park, and the way in which the Park boundary just skirts the other quarrying communities of Bethesda, Llanberis and Nantlle: Llyn Padarn and Dolbadarn Castle, so important in the history of Romantic landscape painting, are actually outside the Park. Again, Eryri looms over the towns of Caernarfon, Bangor, and Beaumaris, whereas the Menai Straits and the hills of Llŷn are inseparable from the most striking views from her summits. The separation of most of the Pembrokeshire Coast from the interior of a county barely thirty miles across, is even more bizarre—the county attracts tourists as a single unit, while its most important economic feature is the natural harbour of Milford Haven. After reorganization, there will still be two separate planning administrations at Haverfordwest, one for the coast and its northern hinterland, the other for the rest of the county. Even here, ignoring every call for good housekeeping and common sense, will the Countryside Council still insist on the principle that a National Park must have a separate Chief Officer and department entirely detached from the new 'unitary' authority?

Many have argued that the Brecon Beacons National Park should be administered by a Board simply because it cuts across the boundaries of four of the eight existing Welsh counties. It would be more sensible to argue that there is little basis for the National Park itself as a planning unit—a unit which extends from the edge of Llandeilo in Dyffryn Tywi to the edge of Abergavenny in Gwent: if pooling expertise was the main consideration, a connoisseur of scenery might as well have extended the Beacons to Grongar Hill, to the Frenni Fawr, and across to Foel Drygarn in the Pembrokeshire Park: but what expertise is necessary in a National Park which is not equally necessary to a county council like Powys or Dyfed in its own right? What values should the National Park uphold which should not also be upheld throughout a unitary authority for Carmarthenshire? The preacher-poet country between, say, Llanwrda and Llanglydwen, celebrated in much minor verse and some classic prose, is too gently and endlessly corrugated to be self-delineating, but is a match for the Moravian hills, the Vysočina, where nature first captivated Mahler. What special care does the town of Brecon in the National Park require which is not also required in Welshpool, where the extensive view of Montgomeryshire from Powis Castle impressed the eighteenth century traveller Lord Lyttleton as 'the most beautiful in South Britain.' Not that the Montgomery District and Powys County planners are in any way inferior to their National Park colleagues: as I travel over the Berwyn into the perfection of north-east Montgomeryshire, I often offer up a prayer that at least this corner of Wales remains undiscovered by the Council for National Parks, unsullied by designation.

DEMOCRACY AND SELF-RESPECT

If Wales is exceptionally beautiful, her people are also—for better or for worse—exceptionally democratic; and exceptionally decentralist. If they are still without a Parliament of their own, even a regional parliament of the type so common, and so successful, within many liberal democracies, this is partly due to an emphasis, from the beginnings of Welsh constitutional law, upon autonomous units much smaller than Wales. Well after the Act of Union introduced us to centralisation, the autonomous congregations of Nonconformity renewed this tradition and served as schools of democracy for the trade unions and voluntary associations of a more secular age. It is no accident that rural Wales produced Robert Owen and Lloyd George. If Saunders Lewis is best remembered for a vision of Wales as a vineyard, a heritage, to be handed down the generations 'in order to keep for the ages to come the beauty which has been,' he too believed a free nation to be 'a community of communities,' freedom to be 'a local thing'. That is one of the differences between European Christian Democracy and the present brand of English Conservatism. The creation of separate National Park Committees, with one third of the members appointed by the Secretary of State, and cutting across communities, is repugnant to the essential Welsh political tradition. From day to day, appointed members can sometimes affect the decisions of a National Park Committee. By and large, however, their very introduction in the role of official custodians of beauty tended to cast their elected colleagues in a different role as custodians of the bread. Add to this the fact that not a few become counter-productive in their zeal, that some are appointed for their political outlook or for their connection with a particular interest like outdoor recreation, and their collective influence becomes a lottery. A body as hybrid as a National Park Committee cannot be accountable either to a local or a national constituency. Even the Review Panel recommended that 'the system for appointments be revised to secure a wider field of high-quality candidates, with greater openness in the process of seeking nominations and making appointments.' Essentially, however, members of committees and boards should represent the public; it is the role of officers to give or secure expert advice. Nothing is more often a matter of opinion than a planning opinion. Yet immodest appointed members sometimes hold themselves out as adequate experts without having had the opportunity to consider the issue in question in professional depth. Some years ago, a Welsh District

Council successfully served an Enforcement Notice on an appointed member of a National Park Committee who had, without permission, erected chalets in a Landscape Conservation Area. He was new to the area but, in view of his previous service as an appointed member of a National Park Board, the Country-side Commission had strongly recommended that the National Park Committee in Wales should have the benefit of his experience. He was, by profession, a planning consultant. He is no longer a member.

The unsatisfactory relationship between a National Park and the normal political community is more than the constitutional absurdity of appointed members being added to bodies which, outside the National Parks, are entirely accountable to the local electorate. Worst of all is the way in which communities, districts and counties are deprived of clear responsibility for the places in which they take the greatest pride. It would be difficult to exaggerate the number or the importance of the evocative scenarios of Welsh history which happen to be within the National Parks. Once, at Penygwryd, I began an after-dinner speech to a mountaineering club dominated by Oxford dons with a reference to the road scheme then threatening Christchurch Meadows: I expressed regret that the fate of the Meadows could not be entrusted to an Oxfordshire National Park Committee to which I myself had been appointed by the Secretary of State, and whose officers were under the thumb of a Countryside Commission based at Caernarfon. They took the point. Since then, we have had the unexpected institution of a Welsh Countryside Council but the CNP and the countryside lobby in general are still blissfully English bodies who regard rural Wales as an outlet for the English conurbations and would like a presumption against any development whatsoever within a National Park.

In the heyday of liberalism, John Stuart Mill himself regarded the West Indies as 'hardly to be looked upon as countries... but more properly as outlying agricultural or manufacuring estates belonging to a larger community... the place where England finds it convenient to carry on the production of sugar, coffee and a few other tropical commodities.' Edward W. Said's influential

Culture and Imperialism shows how the reshaping of the physical environment—making it less foreign, more commodified and, in the process, less evenly developed—is one of the classic features of imperialism, how 'our space at home in the peripheries has been usurped and put to use by outsiders for their purpose,' and how authors like Yeats and Neruda and Césaire have had virtually to recreate their own countries on the map itself. Said draws particular attention to Brian Friel's play *Translations,* which was itself most appropriately translated into and performed in Welsh almost as soon as it appeared in the West End. The play demonstrates how the work of the Ordnance Survey in mapping Ireland between 1824 and 1844—with the exclusion of the Irish from all key and most executive positions, the Anglicization of place-names and the ignoring of traditional boundaries—had the effect of 'defining the Irish as incompetent' and 'depressing their national achievement.' The process was far more subtle and smooth and co-optive, of course, than the Australian equivalent, in which Aborigine languages were ignored and the mapping appeared to have taken place over empty space. It was probably even smoother in Wales, though there can be few richer examples of sublime colonial incomprehension than the 'Nameless Cwm,' which still graces OS Outdoor Leisure Sheet 17 alongside Cwm Cneifion, with the symbols explained in English, French and German, to the exclusion of Welsh; but in Ireland the Survey produced commentaries on 'the state of civilisation and intercourse,' so that the true Welsh equivalent is probably *Brad y Llyfrau Gleision*, the Treason of the Blue Books of 1847. A more academic approach to the mapping of Ireland by the Cambridge scholar Mary Hamer demonstrates that even the rigour of a material survey cannot deliver cartographers from 'the creation of a new fiction.' Indeed Hamer argues that 'an abstracted and standardized representation of terrain' can remove it 'from the cognitive ownership of those who inhabit it.' Is there a connection between the unprecedented prominence given to National Park boundaries by the Ordnance Survey— thick green strips of at least 2mm as opposed to dash-dot county boundaries less decipherable than minor rights of way—and the fact that many Gwynedd people have come to regard the mountains, for fifteen centuries the very essence of Wales, as a playground for the English? It is not as if these artifical boundaries were confined to maps: they extend to a mass of paper and a myriad books. On 28 September, 1994, the Snowdonia National Park Committee formally expressed the wish that the Park be known only as 'Parc Eryri': a cry from the dispossessed, perhaps, rather than from pedants. There are too many parallels for comfort between some aspects of the National Park movement and the lingering, often unconscious, imperialism of some, if by no means all, kinds of England. The precedents suggest that, once Boards have been established, the CNP will want more. According to Said, 'The actual geographical possession of land is what empire in the final analysis is all about.'

BEYOND NATIONAL PARKS: CONSERVING A SMALL NATION

In his recent volume, *Change and Policy in Wales: Wales in the Era of Privatism,* the geographer Richard Prentice, who lectured at University College, Swansea, between 1978 and 1993, concludes: 'The former "reserve" strategies of protecting specific sites or buildings, are… beginning to be seen as inadequate without a wider environmental perspective to sustain them. The post-war legacy of disjointed policies and designations in Wales warrants particular review and revision.' Is it too late to take advantage of both local government reorganization and a new Environment Bill at least to consolidate the three National Parks of Wales, her five Areas of Outstanding Natural Beauty, her Heritage Coast, her Environmentally Sensitive (agricultural) Areas, her Sites of Special Scientific Interest and her National Nature Reserves, together with the Landscape Conservation Areas in county structure plans, the Forest Parks and the many grant-aided forests, into one system which is, on the one hand, coherent and, on the other, democratic? National Trust land and plans should also be considered in this context: the Trust is a statutory, if also a voluntary, body and there should be a Welsh as well as a Scottish National Trust. Under the new system, something akin to National Park legislation and grant-aid could be applied to virtually the whole of rural Wales. But who could take such a bite as that out of local democracy by creating more Boards? The answer is to run the whole system through local government countryside committees. The National Parks would be returned to the new counties as custodians of the national heritage, dispensing in the process with appointed members and the expense of duplicate administration. (In order to keep Snowdonia within one unit, Nant Conwy could be transferred to the new Caernarfon/Meirionnydd county which will contain most of the Park, while all the countryside work of that county could be administered from the present National Park offices at Penrhyndeudraeth.) Most local government committees work within 'national' statutes and standards while, over a wide field, the specific grant was long regarded as the best method of encouraging higher standards. The carrot of grant-aid, tied to development control in manifest accordance with statutory plans, would appeal more effectively to local pride than the division of committees into (inevitably, however good the chairmanship) appointed sheep and elected goats. To the carrot might be added, in the 'national' interest, a stick: the designation of comparatively small areas such as the inner core of Eryri proper, or the Mawddach Estuary proper with Cadair Idris and the Ardudwy peaks, in which no development whatsoever could be permitted without recourse to Parliament, no activity apart from traditional farming and—where ecologically appropriate— traditional mountaineering and walking. This suggestion reflects the recommendation of four members of the Sandford Committee that there should be 'national heritage areas' of supreme landscape value within each National Park. It also accords with international practice and with the IUCN Category III designation, 'Natural Monument/Landmark.' Indeed, it represents the only possibility— admittedly a remote one—of securing in Wales the recognition of internationally recognised Category II National Park, as opposed to Category V 'protected landscape,' which is all that the present National Parks can claim to be, and that somewhat marginally. There is no European Directive on protected landscape but international category might eventually be important from the point of view of grant-aid. No doubt those who administer the present Welsh National Parks will plead the difficulty of choosing and demarcating special areas: but, with the necessary will, it can be done: informally, it is continually being done in the process of development control. County and community councils must be involved in the demarcation, however, and financial compensation must be available to them as well as to owners and occupiers, where appropriate. (See Chapter 20 of the Sandford Report).

The protection of core areas both within and outside the present National Parks should relieve the anxieties of most conservationists about the future of the best known Welsh landscape, and prevent a good deal of time-wasting on the part of developers. At the same time, the prevention of incompatible development by the state must be accompanied by a corresponding statutory obligation to promote compatible, job-creating opportunities, in commerce and industry, or to provide direct financial compensation of the type paid to Anglesey by Shell. Finance must be set aside for this purpose as well as for the promotion, all over Wales, of national park policies such as income support for sustainable farming on the lines of the Tir Cymen scheme: a comprehensive scheme could secure European aid and create about 2,000 jobs. In the context of arguments over the merits of various National Parks, and of Boards as opposed to Committees, it cannot be said too often that the Welsh National Parks have never been as generously financed by central government as their English equivalents. The general threat to the environment requires major changes in priority on the part of the Welsh Office and the Treasury. It also requires administrative changes at the Welsh level so that all rural matters are dealt with by a single department, instead of being divided between several agencies. What is the point of having a Welsh Office if it is not co-ordination? What is the merit of having a Welsh Countryside Council if there is no Welsh Environmental Agency? The

Opposition has rightly demanded that Wales, like Scotland, should have her own environment agency and that, substantially, the two bodies should be merged. At a time when even Swiss cantons like Luzern have integrated their environmental and agricultural and rural development departments, there needs to be a thorough revamp, with only sections like the pollution inspectorate remaining at arm's length from the executive. When one considers how conservation, of all matters, requires public understanding and participation, at a time of diminishing resources, rising standards and ecological crisis, how exasperating it is that there is no Welsh Parliament to which Welsh agencies and departments can account, that county and city government will be even less powerful after reorganisation and that Community Councils—in most liberal democracies the essential tools of civic identification—have such little power! The restoration of democracy to a bureaucratic Wales is beyond the scope of this essay. Unless, however, we progress from conserving particular National Parks to promoting general national pride in the natural, cultural, social and civic heritage of the whole of Wales, and in her European and world responsibilities, those very Parks will eventually succumb to a rising tide of ugliness and pollution.

'Does the land wait the sleeping lord?'

asked David Jones, drawing no doubt on memories of his own sojourn at Capel-y-ffin in the Black Mountains—within the National Park, if it matters—

'Does the land wait the sleeping lord?
or is the wasted land
that very lord who sleeps?'

The sleeping lord is neither Arthur nor Llywelyn but the people of Wales. It is they who must awake and repossess the land, and be themselves possessed by that very land's incomparable diversity.

changing **WALES**

Other titles in the series

Cymru or Wales? R. S. Thomas
The Aesthetics of Relevance Peter Lord
The Democratic Challenge John Osmond
Language Regained Bobi Jones
The Political Conundrum Clive Betts
A Postcard Home Robert Minhinnick
Cardiff: Half-and-half a Capital Rhodri Morgan
The Princeship of Wales Jan Morris